DATE DUE

Demco, Inc. 38-293

HYDROELECTRICITY

Published by Smart Apple Media
1980 Lookout Drive
North Mankato, Minnesota 56003

Design and Production by EvansDay Design

Photographs: Image Finders, JLM Visuals (Lowell
Laudon, John Minnich), Jeff Myers, Tom Myers,
NASA/Kennedy Space Center, Jim Steinberg

LIBRARY OF CONGRESS CATALOGING-IN-PUBLICATION DATA
Gibson, Diane, 1966–
Hydroelectricity / by Diane Gibson.
p. cm. — (Sources of energy)
Includes index.
Summary: Discusses hydroelectricity and how it is
made and used. Includes one simple experiment.
ISBN 1-887068-77-5
1. Hydroelectric power plants—Juvenile literature.
2. Water-power—Juvenile literature. [1. Hydroelectric
power plants. 2. Water power.] I. Title. II. Series.
TK1081 .G513   2000
333.91´4—dc21   99-055894

FIRST EDITION
9 8 7 6 5 4 3 2 1

SOURCES OF ENERGY ....

hydroelectricity

DIANE GIBSON

hydroelectricity

High atop a mountain, snow melts. It trickles down the mountainside, running into other tiny streams. Together, they form a river of water that rushes to the bottom, then empties into a large lake. The water can go no further, though, because the lake is blocked by a large dam. Only a small amount of water is allowed through the dam every day. This water has a special purpose. It is used to create hydroelectricity.

HOLDING BACK WATER

⊙ HYDROELECTRICITY IS PRODUCED at stations called power plants. Most hydroelectric power plants need a dam to hold back the water they use. This water forms a big lake behind the dam. A controlled amount of water is allowed through the dam, helping to produce **electricity** all day and night. ◉ Dams often hold back thousands of tons of water, so they must be very strong. Most dams are made of concrete, which is a mixture of sand, gravel, and a strong type of glue. To make them even stronger, most dams are built with metal rods or wires inside the concrete. ◉ Once a location on a river or lake has been selected for a dam, the water must be held back so that workers can build the dam. Cofferdams are often built for that purpose. These types of dams consist of huge concrete tubes that are sunk into the riverbed or lake bottom until they reach solid rock. The water and sand are then pumped out of the tubes. Cofferdams do not last long; they are used only to keep the ground dry while a permanent dam is being built.

HYDROELECTRIC PLANTS
INCLUDE DAMS THAT HOLD
BACK THE WATER OF LARGE,
DEEP LAKES, OR RESERVOIRS.

AT THE CENTER OF A HYDROELECTRIC PLANT ARE THE GENERATORS, WHICH PRODUCE THE PLANT'S ELECTRICITY.

For strength, all dams are built wider at the bottom than at the top. The deeper the water, the wider the dam must be. Water is used to produce almost all of the electricity used in Norway.

MAKING ELECTRICITY

To GENERATE ELECTRICITY, the water stopped by the dam must be allowed through to the other side at a controlled rate. A sluice gate is lifted (or sometimes lowered, depending on how the dam is built) to let just the right amount of water through. This water hits the blades or paddles of a machine called a turbine, making the turbine spin around. A big pole connects the turbine to a generator, the machine that produces electricity. Inside the generator is a large, round **magnet** that spins around on the pole connected to the turbine. Around the magnet are wires twisted into rings. Electricity is created as the magnet spins inside the wires. This electricity is then carried to homes and other buildings through cables and wires. Workers at the power plant watch the generators to make sure that everything is working right. Big power plants also use computers to monitor the machines. When more electrical power is needed, extra sluice gates are opened and more generators start working.

MOVING WATER HAS GREAT ENERGY. OVER TIME, IT CAN CARVE DEEP CANYONS INTO ROCKY PLAINS.

If water gets too high at a hydro-electric dam, some of it is allowed through a channel called a spill-way. This helps prevent the force of the water from breaking the dam.

By releasing some water, spillways help to lessen the force pressing against dams.

HYDROELECTRIC CHALLENGES

⊙ LIKE ALL ENERGY sources, hydroelectricity does have some drawbacks. One is that people may have to move from their homes if a hydroelectric plant is built nearby. That's because the lakes that form behind dams can get quite big. They often **flood** areas where people and animals once lived, changing the land forever. Power plants that rely on water that comes down a mountain may have problems, too. If the mountain streams dry up, the plants cannot make electricity. To solve this problem, some power plants use pipes to carry water that has gone through sluice gates back up behind the dam. This way, the water can be used again and again. The greatest risk in using hydroelectric power is the breaking of dams. Dams can break if they weaken under the great pressure of the water being held back. They may also break if the rock and earth around them crumble. To guard against this, all dams

WHEN A DAM BREAKS, THE POWER OF THE RUSHING WATER CAN THREATEN LIVES AND PROPERTY.

built today must be strong enough to survive even **earth-quakes** intact. ◎ In 1976, water started trickling from a weak spot in the Teton Dam in Idaho. Fortunately, there was enough time to warn people to leave before it fell apart. Sometimes, however, dams break without warning. Although this rarely happens, it can be disastrous when it does. Dams that suddenly break may kill hundreds of people and damage or destroy any buildings nearby.

THE FAMOUS HOOVER
DAM, ON THE NEVADA-
ARIZONA BORDER,
INCLUDES A HYDRO-
ELECTRIC STATION.

THE LAKES FORMED BEHIND DAMS CAN BE ENORMOUS IN SIZE (DAM IS VISIBLE NEAR TOP OF PHOTO).

Seven of every 10 homes in Canada use hydroelectric power. Lake Mead in Nevada is the largest lake made by a hydroelectric dam. It is about 115 miles (185 km) long.

THE FUTURE OF HYDROELECTRICITY

⦿ MOST DAMMED WATER sources at hydroelectric plants are multi-purpose, used for more than just making electricity. Some of the water in lakes formed behind dams may be sent to water treatment plants. There the water is cleaned and sent to homes for drinking and bathing. Farmers may use some of a dam's water to **irrigate** their crops. People may also use lakes near hydroelectric plants for swimming, fishing, and boating. ⦿ Hydroelectricity has other advantages, too. It doesn't pollute the air as do energy fuels that need to be burned. In addition, water is a renewable source of energy. Some day, we will run out of fuels such as oil, but we will always be able to rely on water. Today, about one-fifth of the world uses hydroelectric power, making it an increasingly popular energy source.

One advantage of hydro-
electricity is that it does
not harm nearby wildlife.

FOR STRENGTH, LARGE DAMS ARE BUILT WIDE AT THE BOTTOM AND GET NARROWER TO- WARD THE TOP.

The Grand Coulee Dam in Washing- ton is one of the world's largest. It stands 550 feet (168 m) high and is 560 feet (170 m) long.

If placed along a stream, a small turbine (with a generator) could generate enough electricity for one house.

MANY DAMS, SUCH
AS THE HOOVER DAM,
DWARF THE POWER
PLANTS AT THEIR BASE.

TO MAINTAIN AN
AMPLE WATER LEVEL,
PLANTS MAY REUSE · · ·
WATER THAT HAS PASSED
THROUGH THE DAM.

The most powerful hydroelectric station in the world is on the Parana River between Brazil and Paraguay. The electricity it produces can light about 120 million light bulbs at the same time.

HISTORY

⊙ HARNESSING THE ENERGY of moving water is not a new development. For thousands of years, people have built waterwheels to help them work. The first waterwheels were made of wood or bamboo, with paddles sticking out around them. When a waterwheel was placed over a moving stream, the water hit the paddles and made the wheel spin around. ❁ Waterwheels were sometimes joined to a saw and used to cut wood. They could also be attached to circular rocks called millstones. One millstone spun around and rubbed against another millstone. Hard corn or wheat was placed between the two stones and ground into flour.

HYDROELECTRIC PLANTS HAVE THEIR ROOTS IN WATER-POWERED GRAIN MILLS OF CENTURIES PAST.

◉ **Build Your Own Dam** You can build your own miniature dam to hold back water. You will need:

> **A deep tray**
> **Water**
> **Sand or dirt**
> **A pencil**

◉ In the middle of the tray, build a wall with the sand or dirt. Now add water to one side. If you made the dam strong enough, the other side of the tray will stay dry.

◉ To see what can happen when a dam breaks, stick a pencil through the wall under the water. When you pull it out, water will spill through. The flow of the water may wear away at the wall until the dam eventually falls apart, filling the whole tray with water.

- **Earthquakes** ARE SUDDEN SHAKINGS OF THE GROUND CAUSED BY SHIFTING ROCK INSIDE THE EARTH.

Electricity IS A TYPE OF ENERGY USED IN HOMES TO RUN LIGHTS AND APPLIANCES.

LAKES AND RIVERS **flood** AREAS WHEN THEIR WATER COVERS LAND THAT IS USUALLY DRY.

FARMERS **irrigate** CROPS BY SUPPLYING THEM WITH WATER BROUGHT IN THROUGH PIPES AND CHANNELS.

A **magnet** IS A PIECE OF METAL THAT ATTRACTS IRON AND STEEL.